CO

For pattern inquiries, please visit: www.go-crafty.com

super fast chevron afghan 》》》

YARN

- 88oz/2500g or 1230yd/1125m of any super bulky weight wool yarn

NEEDLES

- Size 15 (10mm) circular needle, 40"/100cm long *or size to obtain gauge*

LEARN BY VIDEO
www.go-crafty.com

- k1 tbl (knit 1 st through back loop)
- p1 tbl (purl 1 st through back loop)
- pick up and k

》MEASUREMENTS

Approx 65 x 48"/165 x 122cm

》GAUGE

9 sts and 12 rows to 4"/10cm over chevron pat using size 15 (10mm) needle.
Take time to check your gauge.

》NOTE

Circular needle is used to accommodate the large number of sts. Do *not* join. Work back and forth in rows as with straight needles.

》AFGHAN

Cast on 145 sts and work in rib as foll:
Row 1 (WS) *P1, k1; rep from *, end p1.
Row 2 K1 tbl, *p1, k1 tbl; rep from * to end.
Row 3 P1 tbl, *k1, p1 tbl; rep from * to end.

Beg Chevron Pat

Row 1 (RS) Work 12-st rep of row 1 of chart 12 times, work last st of chart.
Cont in pat as established and rep rows 1–12 of chart until 12 rows of chart have been worked 11 times, then work rows 1–6 once more—piece measures approx 47"/119cm from beg.
Next row (RS) K1 tbl, *p1, k1 tbl; rep from * to end.
Next row P1 tbl, *k1, p1 tbl; rep from * to end.
Next row P1 tbl, *k1, p1 tbl; rep from * to end. Bind off loosely in rib.

Side Borders

With RS facing, pick up and k 115 sts evenly along one short edge of afghan. Bind off all sts purlwise on WS. Work in same way along other short edge. ■

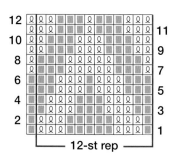

STITCH KEY

- Ω k1 tbl on RS, p1 tbl on WS
- ▦ p on RS, k on WS

checkerboard afghan >>>

> MEASUREMENTS

Approx 43 x 43"/109 x 109cm

> GAUGE

18 sts and 26 rows to 4"/10cm over St st using size 8 (5mm) needles.
Take time to check your gauge.

> NOTE

Circular needle is used to accommodate the large number of sts. Do *not* join. Work back and forth in rows as with straight needles.

> STITCH GLOSSARY

Basketweave Pattern (multiple of 40 sts plus 20)
Row 1 (RS) K20, *p20, k20; rep from * to end.
Rows 2–26 K the knit sts and p the purl sts.
Row 27 P20, *k20, p20; rep from * to end.
Rows 28–52 K the knit sts, and p the purl sts. Rep rows 1–52 for basketweave pat.

> AFGHAN

Cast on 190 sts. K 8 rows.
Next row K5, work basketweave pat to last 5 sts, k5
Cont in pats as established, keeping first and last 5 sts of each row in garter st (k every row) until 52 rows of pat have been worked 5 times. K 8 rows. Bind off. ∎

Paul Amato for LVARepresents.com

triangles & squares afghan »»

❯ MEASUREMENTS

Approx 34 x 60"/86.5 x 152.5cm

❯ GAUGE

12 sts and 18 rows to 4"/10cm over textured pat using size 10½ (6.5mm) needles. *Take time to check your gauge.*

❯ NOTE

Circular needle is used to accommodate the large number of sts. Do *not* join. Work back and forth in rows as with straight needles.

❯ STITCH GLOSSARY

Textured Pattern (multiple of 7 sts)

Row 1 P6, k1.
Row 2 P2, k5.
Row 3 P4, k3.
Row 4 P4, k3.
Row 5 P2, k5.
Row 6 P6, k1.
Rep rows 1–6 for textured pat.

❯ NOTE

Textured pat can be worked foll chart or text.

❯ AFGHAN

Cast on 102 sts.
Row 1 (RS) K2, p to last 2 sts, k2.
Next row Knit.
Next row K2, work row 1 of textured pat 14 times, k2.
Next row K2, work row 2 of textured pat 14 times, k2.
Cont to work textured pat as established, keeping first and last 2 sts in garter st (k every row), until afghan measures 60"/152.5cm from beg, ending with a WS row.
Next row Knit.
Bind off knitwise. ■

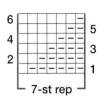

STITCH KEY
☐ k on RS, p on WS
⊟ p on RS, k on WS

Jack Deutsch

windowpane warmth »»

〉YARN 🄸

Any worsted weight cotton yarn
- 35oz/1000g or 1540yd/1410m in cream (A)
- 10½oz/300g or 465yd/420m in red (B)
- 29¾oz/850g or 1190yd/1090m in orange (C)

NEEDLES
- Size 7 (4.5mm) circular needle 47"/120cm long OR SIZE TO OBTAIN GAUGE

NOTIONS
- Bobbins

LEARN BY VIDEO
www.go-crafty.com
- basic intarsia
- seed stitch

〉MEASUREMENTS
55 x 68"/140 x 173cm

〉GAUGE
19 sts and 27 rows to 4"/10cm over St st with B using size 7 (4.5mm) needle.
Take time to check your gauge.

〉NOTES
1 Afghan is worked using circular needles back and forth as if straight needles.
2 Use separate bobbins of yarn for each section of color.
3 Twist yarns on WS to prevent holes.

〉STITCH GLOSSARY
Seed St
Row 1 (WS) *K1, p1; rep from *.
Row 2 (RS) *P1, k1; rep from *.
Rep rows 1 and 2 for seed st.

〉AFGHAN

With A, cast on 220 sts.
Rows 1–7 Work in seed st.
Next row (WS) Work seed st over 5 sts, p 210 sts, inc 15 sts evenly over these 210sts, work seed st over 5 sts—235 sts.
Next row (RS) With A, work seed st over 5 sts, beg chart row 1 rep over next 225 sts. with A, work seed st over last 5 sts.
Keeping first and last 5 sts in A and seed st, work chart rows 1–28 15 times, then work rows 1–7 once.
Next row (WS) With A, work seed st over 5 sts, p 225 sts, dec 25 evenly across the 225 sts, work 5 sts in seed st—220 sts. With A, cont in seed st for 6 rows more. Bind off. ■

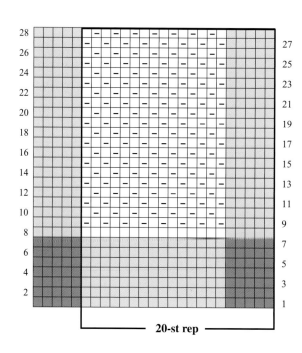

Color Key
- ☐ With A, k on RS; p on WS
- ⊟ With A, p on RS; k on WS
- ▨ With B, k on RS; p on WS
- ▧ With C, k on RS; p on WS

— **20-st rep** —

YARN

Any bulky weight acrylic yarn
- 21oz/595g or 945yd/865m in white (A)
- 27oz/765g or 1215yd/1115m in blue (B)

NEEDLES

Size 15 (10mm) circular needle, 29"/74cm or size to obtain gauge

▶ **LEARN BY VIDEO**
www.go-crafty.com
- basic intarsia
- fringe

〉 MEASUREMENTS

Approx 40 x 56"/101.5 x 142cm

〉 GAUGE

8 sts and 13 rows to 4"/10cm over St st with 2 strands held tog, using size 15 (10mm) needles.
Take time to check your gauge.

〉 NOTES

1 Two strands of yarn are held tog throughout.
2 When changing colors, twist yarns tog on WS to prevent holes.

〉 THROW

Color Sequence 1

Cast on 18 sts A and B, 18 sts with 2 strands A, 18 sts A and B, 18 sts with 2 strands A, 18 sts A and B. Work in St st for 8"/20.5cm, end with a WS row.

Brian Kraus

Color Sequence 2

K 18 sts with 2 strands B, 18 sts A and B, 18 sts with 2 strands B, 18 sts A and B, 18 sts with 2 strands B. Work for 8"/20.5cm, end with a WS row.
Rep color sequence 1 and 2 twice more, then color sequence 1 once more. Bind off.

〉 FINISHING

Cut 11"/28cm lengths of B for fringe. Holding 2 strands tog, fringe all sides. ■

easy entrelac throw 》》》

YARN

- 19¼oz/550g or 1925yd/1760m of any DK weight self-striping wool yarn

NEEDLES

- One pair size 7 (4.5mm) needles *or size to obtain gauge*

▶ LEARN BY VIDEO
www.go-crafty.com

- basic entrelac
- k2tog (knit 2 sts tog)
- k4tog (knit 4 sts tog)
- M1 p-st (Make 1 purl st)
- pick up and k
- pick up and p
- p2tog (purl 2 sts tog)
- sl 1 (slip 1 st)
- ssk (slip, slip, knit, decrease)

》MEASUREMENTS
Approx 27 x 60"/68.5 x 152.5cm

》GAUGE
24 sts and 34 rows to 4"/10cm over St st using size 7 (4.5mm) needles.
Take time to check your gauge.

》STITCH GLOSSARY
M1 p-st Insert LH needle from front to back under the strand between last st worked and the next st on needle. Purl into the back loop to twist the st.

》NOTE
Sl sts purlwise with yarn at WS of work.

Rose Callahan

》THROW
Base Triangles
Cast on 108 sts.
*Row 1 (RS) K2, turn.
Row 2 Sl 1, p1, turn.
Row 3 Sl 1, k2, turn.
Row 4 Sl 1, p2, turn.
Row 5 Sl 1, k3, turn.
Row 6 Sl 1, p3, turn.
Row 7 Sl 1, k4, turn.
Row 8 Sl 1, p4, turn.
Row 9 Sl 1, k5, turn.
Row 10 Sl 1, p5, turn.
Row 11 Sl 1, k6, turn.
Row 12 Sl 1, p6, turn.
Row 13 Sl 1, k7, turn.
Row 14 Sl 1, p7, turn.
Row 15 Sl 1, k8, turn.
Row 16 Sl 1, p8, turn.
Row 17 Sl 1, k9, turn.
Row 18 Sl 1, p9, turn.
Row 19 Sl 1, k10, turn.
Row 20 Sl 1, p10, turn.
Row 21 Sl 1, k11, turn.
Row 22 Sl 1, p11, turn.
Row 23 Sl 1, k11. Do *not* turn.
Rep from * for 8 more triangles—9 triangles made. Turn.

easy entrelac throw >>>

LH Triangle
Row 1 (WS) P2, turn.
Row 2 Sl 1, k1, turn.
Row 3 Sl 1, M1 p-st, p2tog (with last st of triangle and first st of next triangle/rectangle), turn.
Row 4 Sl 1, k2, turn.
Row 5 Sl 1, M1 p-st, p1, p2tog, turn.
Row 6 Sl 1, k3, turn.
Row 7 Sl 1, M1 p-st, p2, p2tog, turn.
Row 8 Sl 1, k4, turn.
Row 9 Sl 1, M1 p-st, p3, p2tog, turn.
Row 10 Sl 1, k5, turn.
Row 11 Sl 1, M1 p-st, p4, p2tog, turn.
Row 12 Sl 1, k6, turn.
Row 13 Sl 1, M1 p-st, p5, p2tog, turn.
Row 14 Sl 1, k7, turn.
Row 15 Sl 1, M1 p-st, p6, p2tog, turn.
Row 16 Sl 1, k8, turn.
Row 17 Sl 1, M1 p-st, p7, p2tog, turn.
Row 18 Sl 1, k9, turn.
Row 19 Sl 1, M1 p-st, p8, p2tog, turn.
Row 20 Sl 1, k10, turn.
Row 21 Sl 1, M1 p-st, p9, p2tog, turn.
Row 22 Sl 1, k11, turn.
Row 23 Sl 1, p11. Do *not* turn.

WS Rectangles
*Pick-up row (WS) Pickup and p 12 sts evenly along edge of next triangle/rectangle, turn.
Row 1 (RS) Sl 1, k11, turn.
Row 2 Sl 1, p10, p2tog, turn.
Rows 3–24 [Rep rows 1 and 2] 11 times more.
Row 25 Rep row 1.
Row 26 Sl 1, p11. Do *not* turn.
Rep from * for 7 more rectangles.

RH Triangle
Pick-up row (WS) Pick up and p 13 sts evenly along edge of last triangle/rectangle, turn.

Row 1 (RS) K13.
Row 2 Sl 1, p9, p2tog, p1, turn.
Row 3 Sl 1, k11, turn.
Row 4 Sl 1, p8, p2tog, p1, turn.
Row 5 Sl 1, k10, turn.
Row 6 Sl 1, p7, p2tog, p1, turn.
Row 7 Sl 1, k9, turn.
Row 8 Sl 1, p6, p2tog, p1, turn.
Row 9 Sl 1, k8, turn.
Row 10 Sl 1, p5, p2tog, p1, turn.
Row 11 Sl 1, k7, turn.
Row 12 Sl 1, p4, p2tog, p1, turn.
Row 13 Sl 1, k6, turn.
Row 14 Sl 1, p3, p2tog, p1, turn.
Row 15 Sl 1, k5, turn.
Row 16 Sl 1, p2, p2tog, p1, turn.
Row 17 Sl 1, k4, turn.
Row 18 Sl 1, p1, p2tog, p1, turn.
Row 19 Sl 1, k3, turn.
Row 20 Sl 1, p2tog, p1, turn.
Row 21 Sl 1, k2, turn.
Row 22 P2tog, p1, turn.
Row 23 K2tog. Do *not* turn—1 st remains.

RS Rectangles
Pick up row (RS) Pick-up and k 11 sts evenly along edge of next triangle/rectangle—12 sts on RH needle, turn.
Row 1 (WS) Sl 1, p11, turn.
Row 2 Sl 1, k10, ssk, turn.
Rows 3–24 [Rep rows 1 and 2] 11 times more.
Row 25 Rep row 1.
Row 26 Sl 1, k11. Do *not* turn.
Pick up row (RS) Pick up and k 12 sts evenly along edge of next rectangle, turn.
Rep from Row 1 eight times more—
9 rectangles made. Turn.
****Work a LH triangle.
Work 8 WS rectangles.
Work a RH triangle.

Work 9 RS rectangles.
Rep from ** 13 more times.
Work a LH triangle.
Work 8 WS rectangles.
Work a RH triangle.

End Triangles
*Pick-up row (RS) Pick up and k 11 sts evenly along edge of next triangle/rectangle—12 sts on RH needle, turn.
Row 1 (WS) Sl 1, p11, turn.
Row 2 K2tog, k9, ssk, turn.
Row 3 Sl 1, p10, turn.
Row 4 K2tog, k8, ssk, turn.
Row 5 Sl 1, p9, turn.
Row 6 K2tog, k7, ssk, turn.
Row 7 Sl 1, p8, turn.
Row 8 K2tog, k6, ssk, turn.
Row 9 Sl 1, p7, turn.
Row 10 K2tog, k5, ssk, turn.
Row 11 Sl 1, p6, turn.
Row 12 K2tog, k4, ssk, turn.
Row 13 Sl 1, p5, turn.
Row 14 K2tog, k3, ssk, turn.
Row 15 Sl 1, p4, turn.
Row 16 K2tog, k2, ssk, turn.
Row 17 Sl 1, p3, turn.
Row 18 K2tog, k1, ssk, turn.
Row 19 Sl 1, p2, turn.
Row 20 K2tog, ssk, turn.
Row 21 Sl 1, p1, turn.
Row 22 K4tog. Do *not* turn—1 st remains.
Rep from * for 8 more triangles. Fasten off last st. ■

quick rib blanket

YARN

YARN 5

- 31½oz/900g or 1080yd/990m of any bulky weight wool yarn

NEEDLES

- One pair size 11 (8mm) needles *or size to obtain gauge.*

❯ MEASUREMENTS

Approx 36 x 70"/91.5 x 177.5cm unstretched

❯ GAUGE

12 sts and 18 rows to 4"/10cm over St st using size 11 (8mm) needles.
Take time to check your gauge.

❯ STITCH GLOSSARY

K2, P2 Rib (multiple of 4 sts)

Row 1 (RS) *K2, p2; rep from * to end.

Row 2 K the knit sts and p the purl sts.

Rep row 2 for k2, p2 rib.

Double Garter Pattern (over any number of sts)

Row 1 (RS) Knit.

Row 2 Knit.

Rows 3 and 4 Purl.

Rep rows 1–4 for double garter pattern.

❯ BLANKET

Cast on 120 sts.

Beg Pat Sequence #1

*[Work 24 sts in k2, p2 rib, work 24 sts in double garter pat] twice, work 24 sts in k2, p2 rib.

Cont in pats as established until 36 rows are complete for pat sequence #1.

Beg Pat Sequence #2

[Work 24 sts in double garter pat, work 24 sts in k2, p2 rib] twice, work 24 sts in double garter pat. Cont in pats as established until 36 rows are complete for pat sequence #2. Rep from * 3 times more, then rep 36 rows of pat sequence #1 once. Bind off. ■

fish scale throw >>>

YARN

- 42oz/1200g or 1440yd/1320m of any bulky weight wool yarn

NEEDLES

- One pair size 9 (5.5mm) needles *or size to obtain gauge*

LEARN BY VIDEO
www.go-crafty.com

- k1 tbl (knit 1 st through back loop)
- sl 1 (slip 1 st)

› MEASUREMENTS

Approx 40 x 60"/101.5 x 152.5cm

› GAUGE

16 sts and 22 rows to 4"/10cm over textured pat using size 9 (5.5mm) needles. *Take time to check your gauge.*

› NOTE

Circular needle is used to accommodate the large number of sts. Do *not* join. Work back and forth in rows as with straight needles.

› STITCH GLOSSARY

Textured Pattern (multiple of 18 sts)
Row 1 K3, p7, k8.
Row 2 P7, k9, p2.
Row 3 K1, p11, k6
Row 4 P5, k4, p5, k4.
Row 5 P3, k7, p3, k5.
Row 6 P5, k2, p9, k2.
Row 7 P1, k11, p1, k5.
Row 8 K6, p11, k1.
Row 9 P2, k9, p7.
Row 10 K8, p7, k3.
Row 11 P4, k5, p4, k5.
Row 12 P6, k3, p5, k3, p1.
Row 13 K2, p2, k5, p2, k7.
Row 14 P8, k1, p5, k1, p3.
Rep rows 1–14 for textured pat.

› NOTE

Textured pat can be worked foll chart or text.

› AFGHAN

Cast on 164 sts.
Row 1 K1 tbl, work row 1 of textured pat 9 times, sl 1 wyif.
Row 2 K1 tbl, work row 2 of textured pat 9 times, sl 1 wyif.
Continue working textured pat as established, keeping first st k1tbl and last st sl 1 wyif, until afghan measures approx 60"/152.5cm, ending with a row 7 or row 14. Bind off. ■

Textured Pattern

14 12 10 8 6 4 2
13 11 9 7 5 3 1

18-st rep

STITCH KEY

☐ k on RS, p on WS

⊟ p on RS, k on WS

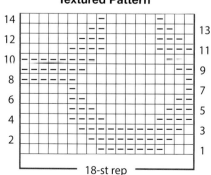

scalloped edge blanket >>>

YARN (6)
- 88oz/2500g or 1230yd/1125m of any super bulky wool yarn

NEEDLES
- Two size 15 (10mm) circular needles, 29"/74cm long *or size to obtain gauge*

NOTIONS
- Small amount of worsted weight yarn for sewing.

LEARN BY VIDEO www.go-crafty.com
- k2tog (knit 2 sts tog)
- p2tog (purl 2 sts tog)
- SKP (Slip 1, Knit 1, Pass slip st over)
- yo (yarn over)

) MEASUREMENTS
Approx 73 x 43"/186 x 109cm

) GAUGE
9 sts and 13 rows to 4"/10cm over St st using size 15 (10mm) needles.
Take time to check your gauge.

) NOTE
Piece is worked back and forth using 2 circular needles to accommodate large number of sts.

) BLANKET
Cast on 123 sts.
Row 1 (RS) Knit.
Row 2 K1, p to the last st, k1.
Rep rows 1 and 2 until piece measures 31"/78.5cm from beg. Bind off.

) EDGING (MAKE 2 STRIPS)
Cast on 253 sts.

Beg Chart
Row 1 (RS) Work first st of chart, then work 18-st rep 14 times across. Cont to foll chart in this manner until row 11 is complete—197 sts.
Note Row 11 is a dec row.
Next row (WS) Knit.
Next row Knit.
Next row (WS) P2, *yo, p2tog; rep from * to last st, p1.
Knit 2 rows. Bind off knitwise.

) FINISHING
With RS of blanket facing and worsted weight yarn, sew short strips of edging tog at one edge to form a long strip. Tack bound-off edge of long strip around entire outer edge of blanket, easing to fit. Sew edging in place. ∎

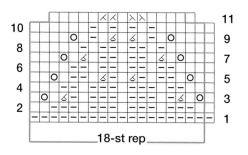

18-st rep

STITCH KEY
- ☐ k on RS, p on WS
- ⊟ p on RS, k on WS
- ⊙ yo
- ◩ k2tog
- ◪ SKP
- ◩ p2tog on RS

14

braided lace afghan »»

YARN ⑤

- 35oz/1000g or 1100yd/1015m of any bulky weight alpaca yarn

NEEDLES

- Size 13 (9mm) circular needle, 47"/120cm long *or size to obtain gauge*

NOTIONS

- Stitch markers

LEARN BY VIDEO
www.go-crafty.com

- k2tog (knit 2 sts tog)
- k3tog (knit 3 sts tog)
- SK2P (Slip 1, Knit 2 tog, Pass slip st over)
- seed stitch
- ssk (slip, slip, knit, decrease)
- yo (yarn over)

〉MEASUREMENTS

Approx 44 x 70"/114 x 177.5cm (blocked)

〉GAUGE

9¼ sts and 12 rows to 4"/10cm over chart pattern, using size 13 (9mm) needle. *Take time to check your gauge.*

〉NOTE

Circular needle is used to accommodate the large number of sts.

〉STITCH GLOSSARY
Seed Stitch (over an even number of sts)

Row 1 *K1, p1; rep from * to end.
Row 2 K the purl sts, and p the knit sts.
Rep row 2 for seed stitch.

〉AFGHAN

Cast on 102 sts. Work in seed st for 5 rows.

Beg Chart

Next row (WS) Work 5 sts in seed st, place marker (pm), work set-up row of chart over center 92 sts, pm, work last 5 sts in seed st. Continue as established until 12 rows of chart have been worked 17 times. Work 5 rows in seed st over all sts. Bind off.

FINISHING

Block gently to open lace pat. ■

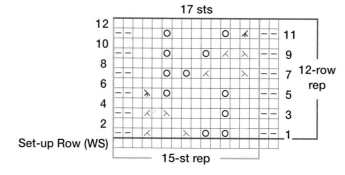

STITCH KEY

- ☐ k on RS, p on WS
- ⊟ p on RS, k on WS
- ▢ yo
- ◩ k2tog
- ◪ ssk
- ◪ k3tog
- ◪ SK2P

cable comfort blanket >>>

YARN (5)

- 26¼oz/750g or 1650yd/1510m of any bulky weight cotton yarn (A)
- 27oz/720g or 1620yd/1480m of any bulky weight mohair yarn in same color as cotton yarn (B)

NEEDLES

- Size 10 (6mm) circular needle, 29"/74cm long *or size to obtain gauge*

NOTIONS

- Size H/8 (5mm) crochet hook
- Cable needle (cn)

LEARN BY VIDEO
www.go-crafty.com

- fringe
- RC (Right Cross)

〉MEASUREMENTS

Approx 42 x 51"/105.5 x 129cm excluding fringe

〉GAUGE

16 sts and 20 rows to 4"/10cm over cable pat using size 10 (6mm) needles and 1 strand A and B held tog.
Take time to check your gauge.

〉NOTE

Use 2 strands held together throughout.

〉STITCH GLOSSARY

6-st RC sl next 3 sts to cn and hold to back, k3, k3 from cn.

〉AFGHAN

With one strand A and B held tog, cast on 169 sts on circular needle. Working back and forth in rows, work cable pat as foll:
Row 1 (RS) K11, *p3, k6; rep from *, end p3, k11.

Row 2 and all even rows K5, p6, *k3, p6; rep from *, end k5.
Row 3 K11, *p3, 6-st RC, p3, k6; rep from *, end p3, 6-st RC, k5.
Row 5 K5, 6-st RC, *p3, k6, p3, 6-st RC; rep from *, end p3, k11.
Rows 7, 9 and 15 Rep row 1.
Row 11 Rep row 5.
Row 13 Rep row 3.
Row 16 Rep row 2. Rep rows 1–16 for cable pat a total of 16 times or 256 rows. Piece measures approx 51"/129cm from beg. Bind off in pat.

〉FRINGE

Cut two 12"/30.5 strands of A for one fringe. With crochet hook, apply fringe to first st on cast-on edge. Cut 2 strands of B and apply fringe to next st. Alternate A and B across cast-on edge then bound-off edge sts. Steam afghan lightly. Trim fringe evenly. ■

easy cable afghan >>>

YARN

- 29¾oz/850g or 1295yd/1185m of any acrylic and wool blend tweed yarn

NEEDLES

- Size 11 (8mm) circular needle 32"/80cm long *or size to obtain gauge*

LEARN BY VIDEO
www.go-crafty.com
- RC (Right Cross)

〉 MEASUREMENTS

Approx 40 x 60"/102 x 152cm

〉 GAUGE

20 sts to 5"/12.5cm and 20 rows to 4"/10cm over cable pat using size 11 (8mm) needles. *Take time to check your gauge.*

Note To make gauge swatch, cast on 20 sts and work in cable pat (following written or charted pat) for 20 rows. Bind off. Piece should measure 5"/12.5cm wide and 4"/10cm long.

〉 STITCH GLOSSARY

10-st RC Sl 5 sts to cn and hold to *back*, k5, k5 from cn.

Cable Pattern (multiple of 20 sts plus 6)

Rows 1, 5, 7, 9 and 11 (RS) *K6, p2, k10, p2; rep from *, end k6.

Rows 2, 4, 6, 8, 10 and 12 P6, *k2, p10, k2, p6; rep from to end.

Row 3 *K6, p2, 10-st RC, p2; rep from *, end k6. Rep rows 1–12 for cable pat.

〉 NOTE

A circular needle is used to accommodate the large number of sts. Work back and forth in rows.

〉 AFGHAN

Cast on 150 sts. Work in garter st (k every row) for 12 rows.

Beg Cable Pat

Row 1 (RS) Cont first 12 sts in garter st, work 20-st rep of cable pat 6 times, work last 6 sts of pat, cont last 12 sts in garter st. Cont in pats as established until piece measures approx 58"/147cm from beg, ending with row 12. Work in garter st over all sts for 12 rows. Bind off all sts loosely. ■

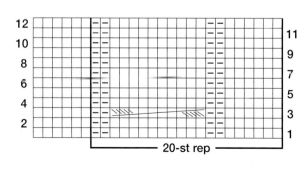

STITCH KEY

☐ K on RS, p on WS

⊟ P on RS, k on WS

▨▨▨ 10-st RC

20-st rep

cozy cable afghan 》》》

YARN
- 35oz/1000g or 2740yd/2505m of any worsted weight wool yarn

NEEDLES
- Size 8 (5mm) circular needle 40"/101.5cm long *or size to obtain gauge*

NOTIONS
- Size G/6 (4.5mm) crochet hook
- Cable needle (cn)

LEARN BY VIDEO
www.go-crafty.com
- LC (Left Cross)
- LT (Left Twist)
- RC (Right Cross)
- RT (Right Twist)
- sc (single crochet)

》 MEASUREMENTS
Approx 40 x 64"/101.5 x 162.5cm

》 GAUGE
21 sts and 27 rows to 4"/10cm over chart 1 or 3 using size 8 (5mm) needles. *Take time to check your gauge.*

》 STITCH GLOSSARY
RT Pass in front of first st and k 2nd st, then k first st and let both sts fall from needle.
LT Pass in back of first st and k 2nd st tbl, then k first st and let both sts fall from needle.
4/4 RPC Sl 4 sts to cn and hold to *back*, k4, sl 1 st from cn back to LH needle, p1, k3 from cn.
4/4 LPC Sl 4 sts to cn and hold to *front*, k4, sl 1 st from cn back to LH needle, p1, k3 from cn.
5/3 RPC Sl 5 sts to cn and hold to *back*, k3, sl 1 st from cn back to LH needle, p1, k4 from cn.
5/3 LPC Sl 5 sts to cn and hold to *front*, k3, sl 1 st from cn back to LH needle, p1, k4 from cn.
9-st LPC Sl 6 sts to cn and hold to *front*, k3, sl 3 sts from cn back to LH needle, p3, k3 from cn.
11-st LPC Sl 7 sts to cn and hold to *front*, k4, sl 3 sts from cn back to LH needle, p3, k4 from cn.

Cluster St
Yo, insert hook into next st and draw up a lp, yo and draw through 2 lps on hook, [yo, insert hook into same st and draw up a lp, yo and draw through 2 lps] 3 times, yo and draw through all lps on hook.

STITCH KEY
- ⊟ K on RS, p on WS
- ☐ P on RS, k on WS
- ⊠ RT
- ⊠ LT
- ⬚ 4/4 RPC
- ⬚ 4/4 LPC
- ⬚ 5/3 RPC
- ⬚ 5/3 LPC
- ⬚ 9-st LPC
- ⬚ 11-st LPC

Chart 1
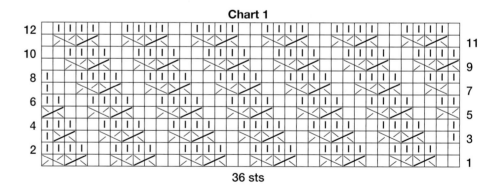
36 sts

Chart 3
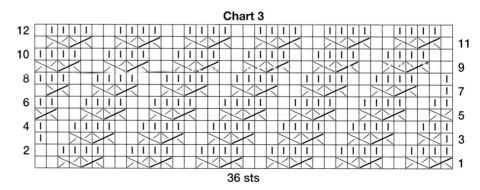
36 sts

cozy cable afghan »»

) AFGHAN

Cast on 219 sts.

Beg Chart Pats

Row 1 (RS) *Work 36 sts chart 1, 25 sts chart
2, 36 sts chart 3*, 25 sts chart 2; rep from *
to * once. Cont in pat as established until 60
rows of chart 2 have been worked 7 times,
then work 6 rows more. Bind off in pat.

) FINISHING

Block piece to measurements.

Edging

With RS facing and crochet hook, work 1 rnd
sc around entire afghan.
Next rnd Ch 2, work partial cluster (work
between [ ] twice instead of 3 times) in next
st, *ch 1, skip 1 st, work cluster in next st;
rep from * around. Work 2 more rnds in sc.
Fasten off. Block edging. ■

STITCH KEY

Symbol	Meaning
I	K on RS, p on WS
☐	P on RS, k on WS
⧄	RT
⧅	LT
	4/4 RPC
	4/4 LPC
	5/3 RPC
	5/3 LPC
	9-st LPC

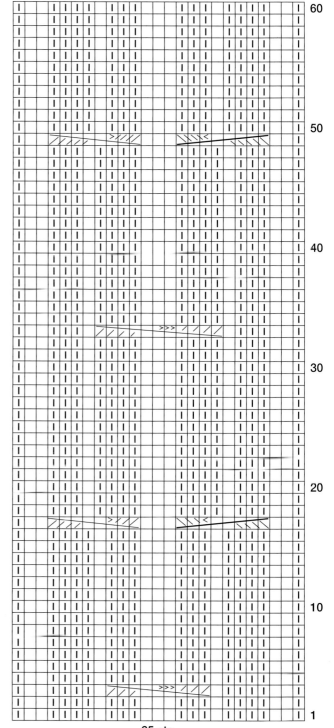

Chart 2

25 sts